DOXIE MOXIE

DOXIE MOXIE

Little Dog BIG Attitude

WILLOW CREEK PRESS

Published by Willow Creek Press
P.O. Box 147, Minocqua, Wisconsin 54548

For information on other Willow Creek Press titles,
call 1-800-850-9453

Photo Credits: p2 © Jean Michel Labat/Ardea.com; p6 © Randy Handwerger/RandyProductions.com; p8 © Sally Weigand; p11 © Ron Kimball/ronkimballstock.com; p12 © Tara Darling; p15 © Norvia Behling; p16 © Tara Darling; p19 © Bonnie Nance; p20-28 © Norvia Behling; p31 © Cheryl A. Ertelt; p32 © BIOS Klein J.-L. & Hubert M.-L./Peter Arnold; p35 © Norvia Behling; p36 BIOS/Peter Arnold; p39 © Diane Calkins/Click the Photo Connection; p40 © Jean Michel Labat/Ardea.com; p43 © Cheryl A. Ertelt; p44 © Cris Kelly; p47 © Brenda Hawkes; p48 © Sharon Eide/Elizabeth Flynn; p51 © Rosemary Shelton/Click the Photo Connection; p52 © Bonnie Nance; p55 © Norvia Behling; p56 © www.jeanmfogle.com; p59-60 © Norvia Behling; p63 © www.jeanmfogle.com; p64 © Bonnie Nance; p67 © Norvia Behling; p68 © Ulrike Schanz/AnimalsAnimals; p71 © Rosemary Shelton/Click the Photo Connection; p72 © Cris Kelly; p75 © Tara Darling; p76 © Dale & Kerrin Church/ronkimballstock.com; p79 Carolyn A. McKeone/Photo Researchers, Inc; p80 © Norvia Behling; p83 © Londie G. Padelsky; p84,87 © Tara Darling; p88 © Sue Redshaw; p92 © Norvia Behling; p95 © Randy Handwerger/RandyProductions.com

Printed in Canada

Dear reader,

In an effort to validate my points, I have enlisted the thoughts of notable intellectuals, including the writings of German philosophers, playwrights, and scholars. You will also find, sprinkled among my own insights, the age-old wisdom of German proverbs as well as the musings of a favorite poet, Henry Wadsworth Longfellow. I would also like to thank Melissa Sovey for transcribing my cogitations and for realizing the significance of spreading the word on doxie moxie (once she realized that dachshunds don't really appreciate being told "no").

Sincerely,

Herr Schnapps Hamm

Never let it be said
that dachshunds are not well-read.   – Schnappsie Hamm

Okay people, first off we don't like being snickered at and called "weiner dogs." We're long and low-slung because we have a proud heritage of tunneling and crawling through holes to chase badgers. Have you ever had a smackdown with an angry badger in the dark? If not, you have no idea of our spirit, courage and tenacity. So stop the name-calling.

Because there's probably a whole lot of other things you don't know about us, we've put this little book together in alphabetical order to give you the long and short of what it takes to be a dachshund, or if you prefer, "doxie."

Doxie moxie is all about being full of spirit, full of gumption and unabashedly full of oneself.

Animated

Of course, there's always room for more self-fulfillment ... so do slather on the attention.

We doxies pride ourselves on our tubular configuration which allows little wind resistance and maximum speed... we'll have that squirrel faster than you can say "lederhosen."

Aerodynamic

...let's see a pug do this!

A dachshund knows of everyone's comings and goings in his yard and will **NOT TOLERATE** trespassers (except for the occasional Garden Gnome). Highly regarded as fearless hunters, even giant bunnies won't escape our wrath.

Brazen

Did some bunny say hasenpfeffer????????

In an effort to live up to our Bavarian heritage of near obsessive cleanliness, we will eagerly jump in the tub. Well, we also know that the couch is off limits until we do.

Clean

Lieber Staub aufwirbeln als Staub ansetzen.
It's better to raise the dust than to get dusty.
– Hubert Burda

Known for our superior intelligence, and our very dexterous snouts, dachshunds will charm you with adroitness. Really... we'll just help ourselves.

Clever

What the lion cannot manage to do the fox can.
- German Proverb

Yes, doxies have great minds AND multi-faceted interests...
including provocative bunny luring techniques.
Word of advice, sometimes it's better not to ask...

Complicated

Only one man ever understood me,
and he didn't understand me.

- Georg Wilhelm Friedrich Hegel

We are a tad driven to dig... okay it's more like a rigorous religious devotion, but hey, this was bred into us. It's certainly not an addiction or anything. (I ought to know, I've been doing it for years)

Compulsive

He who is firm in will molds the world to himself.
- Johann Gottlieb

Of course, digging is a fine method of exercise. You should most definitely recognize the fact that the dachshund is a **GOURMAND EXTRAORDINAIRE**. Our reputation for over-indulgence however, should not keep you from sharing.

Connoisseur

I'm not a glutton – I'm an explorer of food.

- Erma Bombeck

Indeed, maintaining our sleek physique is imperative for those times when hiding from you is in our best interest...

Covert

...or when we have had enough of the crazy household and we simply "vant to be alone."

Our inquiring minds often lead to tight spots... and spots of trouble. Please know that although we are fond of displaying airs of complete self-reliance, we do occasionally need your assistance even though this is hard to admit.

Curious

Did you ever walk into a room and forget why you walked in? I think that's how dogs spend their lives.

- Sue Murphy

True doxie moxie: convincing you that no matter the size of the catastrophe we have caused, we are always deserving of treats and your unconditional love. And, since we are the masters of THE STARE DOWN, you might as well give it up.

Demanding

The demand to be loved is the greatest
of all arrogant presumptions.
- Friedrich Nietzsche

That's right, WE NEVER give up when we are after something.
What's moxie if not fierce stick-to-itiveness?????

Determined

When you are thwarted, it is your
own attitude that is out of order.
- Meister Eckhart

Our limitless determination makes us enthusiastic playmates. Fetch? Well, we'll CHASE balls all day. We just don't see the need to bring them back to you... how very tedious.

Eager

Isn't life not a thousand times
too short for us to bore ourselves?

- Friedrich Nietzsche

After all folks, it's **ALL ABOUT US**... right?

Egotistical

If we were not all so interested in ourselves, life would be so uninteresting that none of us would be able to endure it.

– Arthur Schopenhauer

Should you forget that **EVERYTHING** revolves around your doxie, and you are still withholding (or scolding for some minor infraction), know this... we may not always get our way, but we'll make sure you **FEEL THE GUILT.**

Expressive

He speaketh not; and yet there lies
A conversation in his eyes.
- Henry Wadsworth Longfellow

In fact, we may even threaten to leave or shun you forever. Please note that we have also perfected the moxie-art of THE LOOK.

Fickle

When rejected by his father he became industrious and motivated; when rejected by his mother he became proudly independent; when rejected by his siblings he became deeply compassionate; but when rejected by the family dachshund he became a complete nut case.

– from an alleged case history of Sigmund Freud

But not to worry, we're pretty level-headed and forgiving. We'll never worry that you won't come around and succumb to our ploys. Remember an important rule, there's nothing a little EXTRA attention can't remedy.

Grounded

He who prizes the little things is worthy of great ones.
- German Proverb

Once we feel confident that you now understand the rules, we'll be back to our old **ÜBER COOPERATIVE** selves. You'll often find us in the midst, literally, of a pile of chores.

Helpful

Sorting your laundry for instance...

...or straightening the bed.

If you're REALLY good, we may even offer to take YOU for a ride... as long as you realize it's OUR WAY or THE HIGHWAY.

Independent

You have your way. I have my way. As for the right way, the correct way, and the only way, it does not exist.

– Friedrich Nietzsche

As long as we are given the recognition we deserve, there's no end to the LENGTHS and HEIGHTS a doxie will go for you. Did I mention that we are valiant, chivalrous and stout-hearted???

Intrepid

Lassie's got nothin' on us.

Your doxie is the ONLY inhabitant of the house that is allowed to make lots of noise at will. Please note that vacuuming is VERBOTTEN between the hours of 9:00am and 5:00pm as these are prime napping hours.

Loud

I have long held the opinion that the amount of noise that anyone can bear undisturbed stands in inverse proportion to his mental capacity and therefore must be regarded as pretty fair measure of it.

- Arthur Schopenhauer

Yes, we have attitude and spunk, but we also know when it's time to suck up a bit and remind you of our devotion.

Loyal

For instance, the "I'm so sorry to be underfoot but I think you dropped something" routine works like a charm.

Doxie moxie has a soft and sweet side as well.
Endearing looks and perfect backdrops add
a dramatic flair to the "irresistible act."

Manipulative

Don't accept your dog's admiration as
conclusive evidence that you are wonderful.

– Ann Landers

And on the tougher side, it's still all about image.
Our barrel-chested anatomy comes naturally,
yet we always keep props handy...

Muscled

...just in case unexpected company necessitates a little flexing.

Fortunately, developed pecs make tugging and shredding less physically taxing. And rigorous cardiac training allows us to run faster than you.

Mischievious

The price of inaction is far greater than the cost of making a mistake.
– Meister Eckhart

Speaking of the occasional indiscretion, doxies have an unfair association as a difficult breed to housebreak. Hey, with legs like this, do you really expect us to go out in that weather? Besides, this is RECYCLING!

Naughty

We judge ourselves by what we feel capable of doing, while others judge us by what we have already done.
– Henry Wadsworth Longfellow

You see, a doxie with moxie realizes that it's very important
to keep you THINKING that we are difficult to train.
That way, we retain our self-respect with the added bonus of
watching you scramble for more irresistable treats.

Nonconforming

A rule of thumb obvious to all doxies is that
the harder you have to work to get us to do
something, the bigger and better the reward.

Really, it's hard to imagine what some dogs are thinking, performing little tricks and being of service to others for next to nothing. Yes, for the dachshund, life is all about reaping the rewards while letting OTHERS do the work.

Opportunistic

From the first day to this, sheer greed
was the driving spirit of civilization.
- Freidrich Engels

However, in moments of PURE ALTRUISM, we have been known to share our witty conversational skills...

Outgoing

...and our supreme company with "lesser" creatures.

We've even been known to politely tolerate
your boring puppy talk...

Patient

... though this can be a formidable task for the young and
inexperienced doxie still working on his moxie.

Unfortunately, the more mature among us have a tendency to get carried away with our pride... fueled by your constant praise and attention (not our fault). This often results in an unrestrained need to remind others of their place in the household. This works better on the cat and the chihuahua however.

Rash

Some are made modest by
great praise, others insolent.
– Friedrich Nietzsche

It is no small wonder that we tend to look down our noses at others. This is obviously genetically predisposed, and therefore another issue where we should not be held accountable.

Snooty

You say my nose, sir, reminds you of a dachshund?
That is the first flattering remark anyone has made of it.
– Cyrano de Bergerac

We were born to mix with HIGH BROWS...

Sophisticated

. . .and to flaunt our fashion sense.

Some might confuse our haughtiness
with obstinate doggedness.

Stubborn

Some day, if I ever get a chance, I shall write a book, or
warning, on the character and temperament of the
dachshund and why he can't be trained and shouldn't be.
I would rather train a striped zebra to balance an Indian club
than induce a dachshund to heed my slightest command.

– E.B. White

(Well, maybe you should have E.B., instead of writing about
little mice and pigs and spiders and the proper use of adverbs.)

In reality we're just making sure EVERYONE understands who's boss and who's got more moxie. Sometimes this takes persistence. (Told you this works better on the chihuahua).

Tenacious

At times one remains faithful to a cause only because its opponents do not cease to be insipid.
– Friedrich Nietzsche

Yes, doxies have been known to attract the limelight, and to revel in it. We have shared Hollywood homes with the likes of John Wayne and Carol Lombard, both of whom honed their crafts under our scrupulous direction.

Theatrical

Fame comes only when deserved, and then is as inevitable as destiny, for it is destiny.

- Henry Wadsworth Longfellow

Our flair for the stage and our star-of-the-show
moxie keeps our performing talents sharp.

Tolerant

We'll even indulge your silly whims
with compassion and patience...

...until we decide the insanity has gone far enough.

We do not have to visit a madhouse to find disordered
minds; our planet is the mental institution of the universe.
– Johann Wolfgang von Goethe

That's right. A doxie will always be truthful with you. Brutally. Honest as the day is long, we may refuse to go for a walk with you until you replace your limburger-smelling garden boots with an airier walking shoe.

Upright

We are scent hounds after all.

Other superlatives aside, and with all due respect to our canine brethren, I'm sure you will agree that **DACHSHUNDS** deserve the **HIGHEST** respect and esteem.

Venerable

Given our wisdom and superiority, please also remember that we have certain **RULES** we expect our "domestic partners" to follow. For instance, **WE DECIDE** if there is any room for you, once **WE** are under the covers.

Yes indeed, there's no finer breed than the dachshund.

Wonderful

(note: HUMBLE was deliberately left out of this book.)

So there you have it folks. My hope is that this little primer has brought you up to speed on the true essence of **DOXIE MOXIE**. Now that we've cleared some things up, and we are all on the same page, so to speak, let me add an important afterward.

Doxie moxie may be all about our **ALL-ABOUT-ME TEMPERAMENT**, but I'll just go ahead and admit that we couldn't pull it off without you! Sure, we've got attitude, but we also know that as much as we try to hide it, we have an almost irresistible urge to be a part of everything you do. I guess you probably know that though.

Yes, we love you too...